Jeanne M. Lesinski

Lerner Publications Company
Minneapolis

To my mother, who helped me buy my first computer

This book is available in two bindings:
Library binding by Lerner Publications Company
Softcover by First Avenue Editions
Divisions of Lerner Publishing Group
241 First Avenue North
Minneapolis, MN 55401 U.S.A.

Website address: www.lernerbooks.com

Library of Congress Cataloging-in-Publication Data

Lesinski, Jeanne M.
    Bill Gates / by Jeanne Lesinski.
       p.   cm.—(A&E biography)
    Includes bibliographical references.
    Summary: A biography of the man who created Microsoft, from his childhood to his battle in court after being accused of having a monopoly in the computer industry.
    ISBN 0–8225–4949–2 (alk. paper).
    ISBN 0–8225–9689–X (pbk. : alk. paper)
    1. Gates, Bill, 1955–   —Juvenile literature. 2. Businessmen—United States—Biography—Juvenile literature. 3. Computer software industry—United States—History—Juvenile literature. 4. Microsoft Corporation—History—Juvenile literature. [1. Gates, Bill, 1955–   .
2. Businessmen. 3. Computer software industry. 4. Microsoft Corporation—History.] I.Title.
HD696.63.U62G3745 2000
388.7'610053'092—dc21
    [B]   99–34009

Manufactured in the United States of America
1 2 3 4 5 6 – JR – 05 04 03 02 01 00

CONTENTS

As owner of Microsoft Corporation, Bill likes a casual work atmosphere in the office. Here, he relaxes while being interviewed in March 1991.

INTRODUCTION

BILLIONAIRE COMPUTER TYCOON. RUTHLESS COMPETI-
tor. Astute predictor of future technology. Lucky.

People have called Bill Gates many names. But they
may not see the Bill Gates who fell in love with computers when he was thirteen years old. He has never
fallen out of love.

Bill hasn't forgotten how he felt when he first
encountered computers. In January 2000, he announced that Steve Ballmer, longtime friend and
coworker at Microsoft Corporation, would become the
company's new CEO (chief executive officer). Ballmer
would handle many of the day-to-day management
responsibilities for Microsoft. That way, Bill could
return to his first love—creating new products. Bill

The promotion of Steven Ballmer, right, *was part of Bill's plan to broaden Microsoft's leadership.*

would work with development teams throughout the company to create software and computer services to meet the customers' needs.

"Microsoft is almost a quarter-century old, but we are just at the beginning," Bill wrote in a September 1998 memo to Microsoft employees. "The future makes me very excited about my job and working with all of the Microsoft team to continue to surprise the world with our achievements. We can all be incredibly proud of what we've built so far. But the future opportunities will far surpass everything we've achieved to date. I'm more enthusiastic about and committed to Microsoft than I've ever been."

Bill has quipped more than once that if his parents had known that he would become famous, they wouldn't have given him the name of his father—William Henry Gates. They would have given him a unique name to match his unique status. But how could the Gateses have known that their small and shy son would build a company from two employees to more than thirty thousand? How could they have known that he would lead a far-reaching technological revolution—or that he would become the richest man in the world?

Mary Gates, left, often took Bill, right, along when she made presentations at various schools in Seattle, Washington.

Chapter **ONE**

GROWING UP

AFTER SERVING IN THE ARMY IN **W**ORLD **W**AR **II**, Bill Gates's father, William Gates II, studied law at the University of Washington in Seattle. There, he fell in love with a charming and energetic education student, Mary Maxwell. The two married in 1951 and settled in the View Ridge neighborhood in Seattle. William, who went by the name Bill, joined a law firm in Seattle. Mary taught at area schools.

The couple's first child was born in 1953, a daughter named Kristianne. Two years later, on October 28, 1955, William Henry Gates III joined the family. His younger sister, Libby, was born in 1964.

Right away, "Little Bill" demonstrated good humor and high energy, rocking in his cradle. Later, he grew particularly fond of a rocking horse, which he would ride for hours. Little Bill discovered that rocking improved his ability to think—and think he did.

At school, Bill was the youngest student in his class. Though he was small for his age and somewhat clumsy, he shined academically. Certain subjects, such as math and science, were easy for him. Bill read voraciously. He read entire textbooks in the first few days of class. He entered and won summer reading contests at the local public library.

At age eight, Bill started to read the 1960 edition of the *World Book Encyclopedia.* "I was determined to read straight through every volume," he recalled. By the time he reached the entries under the letter *P,* Bill discovered a more detailed encyclopedia and decided he would never have enough time or patience to read the entire new set.

Mary Gates recalled that her son was always thinking. "He'd never ever be ready when we were going someplace, and we'd call out to him, 'What are you doing?'" Bill would answer, 'Thinking.' Bill even chided his parents, asking, "Don't you ever think?"

"We didn't have a good answer to that," Bill Gates Sr. added. "We weren't sure we ever did."

Intelligent and energetic, Mary Gates worked with volunteer organizations in her community and rose to national leadership positions. Since Mary was so busy, her mother, Adelle Maxwell (nicknamed "Gam"), cared for the grandchildren after school. When Bill and his

Bill's father in the mid-1990s

sisters came home from school, Gam met them with snacks and activities.

Weeknight television was not allowed, but reading and games were household staples. Board games, puzzles, and card games went on for hours. Gam loved card games and taught the children to play bridge. She nicknamed Bill "Trey," after the cardplayer term for three and because he was William Henry Gates III.

Bill Gates Sr. recalled that after dinner on Sundays, the entire family would gather to play games. "The play was quite serious. Winning mattered," Bill's father remembered. Fiercely competitive, Trey didn't like to lose.

When Bill was in fourth grade, the family moved to a new home in the Laurelhurst area of Seattle. By this time, Bill was bored with school. He applied himself in the subjects he liked—math and reading—but made little effort at those that he found boring. Left-handed, Bill sometimes took notes with his right hand, just to give himself a little challenge when bored in class.

At the Laurelhurst Elementary School library, Bill worked to find wrongly shelved and lost books, a job that demonstrated his diligence and attention to detail. Sometimes the teachers had to make him stop working and go out for recess. In the library, Bill discovered the work of Leonardo da Vinci, a scientist and artist who lived in Italy from 1452 to 1519. When asked about his future career, Bill answered that he wanted to be a scientist.

At times, people thought Bill was a goof-off or class clown because he didn't seem to pay attention in school. He would make wisecracks and sometimes argue with teachers. His parents thought he was a dramatic underachiever. They wanted him to respect the educational process.

Bill was not interested in team sports. He tried Little League baseball, but the pace was too slow for him. He found roller-skating, tennis, and skiing—both on snow and water—to be more exciting. In summer he hung out at the Laurelhurst Beach Club, where he could swim, dive, and sail on Lake Washington. The family rented rustic cabins on the Hood Canal near

Puget Sound. There, they would gather with friends for picnics, games, and campfires. Bill also joined a Boy Scout troop, where fun was foremost and formality nowhere to be found. With its hiking and camping trips, the troop fed Bill's craving for adventure.

The Gates family regularly went to services at the University Congregational Church. When challenged by the church pastor to memorize the Sermon on the Mount, Bill flawlessly recited this lengthy passage from the Bible. For his effort, he won a free dinner at the Space Needle, a famous Seattle landmark, compliments of the pastor.

FINDING A FOCUS

During sixth grade, Bill still lacked a focus for his intellect. "My desk was always messy, and I didn't seem to be paying attention. I was always out there on the playground trying to form some sort of group of guys, or sort of laughing about something when you weren't supposed to be laughing," he remembered. Bill did find satisfaction with one school group, the Century Club, made up of bright sixth graders. With the Century Club, Bill went on educational field trips, played board games, and discussed books and current events.

He did well in a special economics class at school. For the class, he created a fictitious business report called "Invest with Gatesway Incorporated." Bill imagined himself as a young inventor who manufactured and marketed a new product.

Bill and Mary Gates became concerned about their son when he was ready for junior high. "He was so small and shy, in need of protection, and his interests were so very different from the typical sixth grader's," his father remembered. The Gateses debated whether or not to send their underachieving son to a private school, where class sizes would be smaller and disci-

As an eighth grader, Bill, left, *was smaller than many of his peers.*

pline more stringent. They wanted their son to learn good study habits. They wanted him to prepare for college and a career. Finally, they decided to send Bill to Lakeside School, an exclusive boys' school in Seattle for students in grades seven through twelve. There students wore jackets and neckties, carried briefcases, and had assigned seating—even at lunch.

The first year, 1967, Bill tried to adjust to his new school and schoolmates. He still didn't work hard. He was a B student, except in honors algebra, in which he earned an A minus. He hung out with other students interested in math and science. As usual, he read a lot, including biographies of the French emperor Napoleon Bonaparte and American president Franklin D. Roosevelt.

When Bill and the other students started math and science classes in 1968, they discovered an intriguing new machine in Lakeside's McAlister Hall. It was a Teletype machine, made up of a keyboard, a printer, and a paper-tape punch and reader. The machine could be hooked up to a telephone by placing the receiver in a special cradle. Through the telephone lines, the Teletype machine communicated with a computer at a local General Electric office.

At this time, in the late 1960s, personal computers had not yet been invented. Instead, businesses and universities used mainframe computers that were bigger than refrigerators. Holes punched in paper tapes instructed the computers to perform mathematical calculations and other tasks. Researchers at universities and laboratories used the computers to analyze data. Businesses, such as electric companies, used computers to calculate and print monthly bills for customers.

Mainframe computers cost many millions of dollars, so many businesses and universities often shared a single mainframe. Users at different locations made paper tapes carrying instructions. Using Teletype machines and telephone lines, users sent the instructions to the mainframe computer they shared with others.

At first the Lakeside students did not know a thing about computers—and their teachers didn't know much more. But, like a complex puzzle, the computer gave feedback and information. If the user correctly wrote instructions, called programs, the computer responded with solutions to mathematical questions. If a program wasn't written correctly, it couldn't produce useful responses.

To Bill, the computer was a challenge to be mastered. Describing his first encounter with the computer, Bill recalled, "I wrote my first . . . program when I was thirteen years old. It was for playing tic-tac-toe. The computer I used was huge and cumbersome and slow and absolutely compelling." Bill had found his focus.

Since the school had no formal course in computing, teachers and students alike taught themselves from computer manuals. Bill and other students spent as much time as they could using the computer. They learned different programming languages, each with its own particular rules and vocabulary. These languages included BASIC—Beginner's All-purpose Symbolic Instruction Code—and FORTRAN, a programming language used by scientists.

The students wrote simple programs—also called software—which grew in size and complexity. Bill wrote a program to play the game Risk using a computer. In this game, players pretend to take over the world. Another student wrote a program to calculate grade-point averages using the computer.

This mainframe computer has various components. The storage units are the tall towers at the bottom left.

Bill worked in the computer room so much that some other students complained that he was hogging the equipment. These same students often came to Bill for answers when they got stuck with programming problems.

In ninth grade, Bill's school performance changed dramatically. "I came up with a new form of rebellion," he explained. "I hadn't been getting good grades, but I decided to get all As without taking a book home. I didn't go to math class, because I knew enough and had read ahead, and I placed within the top ten people in the nation on an aptitude exam. That established my independence and taught me I didn't need to rebel anymore." Bill became a straight-A student.

Bill in Lakeside School's computer room. Note the Teletype type-writer in the lower left corner.

At home, his room was a jumble of paper computer tapes, dirty clothes, and reading material. After trying various ploys to get Bill to clean his room, his parents decided to close the door on the mess.

General Electric charged the Lakeside students $89 per month for the Teletype and $8 an hour for computer time. At these rates, the computer students quickly racked up enormous bills. The Lakeside Mothers' Club helped fund their computer use through an annual garage sale, but the students needed to find other ways to pay for computer time.

While Bill's parents paid his school tuition and bought his books, they insisted he pay for his own computer fees. "This is what drove me to the commercial side of the software business," Bill explained. He wanted to work with computers and get paid for it.

Another influence was Bill's best friend, Kent Evans. Kent was very interested in both computers and the business world, and he exuded confidence that was unusual for someone his age. For a time, he and Bill were inseparable. "We read *Fortune* [business magazine] together; we were going to conquer the world," Bill said.

The Lakeside computer students were elated when Computer Center Corporation opened their business in Seattle. The company owned a mainframe computer, and the Lakeside students hooked up to it using a Teletype machine and phone lines. Because so few people understood computers in those years, the company director decided to rely on the Lakeside students for help.

The students worked during the company's off hours, testing the computer and fixing bugs or flaws in the programs. Students caught buses from Lakeside to "C-Cubed" (as the company was soon dubbed for the three "Cs" in its title) and stayed there for hours. Sometimes Bill sneaked out of his room at night to go work on the computer. If he missed the last bus, he'd have to walk three miles home.

Eventually C-Cubed went out of business. Undeterred, Bill and some other students, among them upperclassman Paul Allen, found weekend and summer jobs writing programs for other computer companies. Computer programs are written in steps. The first step is to develop the process for solving a problem. The next step is to write "code"—a program that will solve the problem. Gates and Allen wrote computer code in return for free computer time as well as for payment.

Bill also took a job with a company that was analyzing traffic patterns. Using hoses laid across highways, the company collected data about traffic use. Bill took charge of counting the data and putting it into a computer at the University of Washington. He hired several Lakeside students to help count, while he input the data by punched tape. Then he printed out the results.

During Bill's junior year, Lakeside merged with St. Nicholas, an all-girls' school. With more students— about five hundred—the class schedule was difficult to determine by hand. Each of the students attended eight classes a day. Some classes met only one day a week. Some classes included an extra two-hour laboratory period.

Several teachers tried to write a computer program to create the schedule, but they couldn't do it on their own. They tapped Bill and his friend Kent Evans for help. The two boys spent long hours at the task, often going without much-needed sleep. As the deadline neared, tragedy struck. Kent fell to his death in a mountaineering accident.

Bill was devastated. "I had never thought of people dying," he remembers. He was supposed to speak at Kent's memorial service, but he was too upset to do so. "For two weeks I couldn't do anything at all," Bill wrote. After some time, Bill continued to work on the scheduling program. He and Paul Allen eventually finished it.

During Bill's senior year, he and Paul, who had already graduated, took programming jobs with the engineering firm TRW, Inc. in Vancouver, Washington. The company was writing a computer program that would control the Bonneville Power Administration's electricity distribution grid. School officials gave Bill permission to miss classes so he could attend work. The job was considered his senior project.

The duo also tried to build their own special-purpose computer and software. Computer chips—the brains of a computer—were very primitive during this time,

With Bill looking on, Paul Allen types at the keyboard of the ASR-33 Teletype machine at Lakeside School in 1968.

so Gates and Allen tried to think of a simple job for their machine. They came up with Traf-O-Data, a system to count and analyze traffic patterns.

Although they were never able to finish the project, their friendship grew as they worked together. "I was lucky in my early teens to become friends with Paul Allen," Bill once remarked. "Paul had lots of answers to things I was curious about. . . . I was more of a math person than Paul, and I understood software better than anyone he knew. We were interactive resources for each other. We asked or answered questions, drew diagrams, or brought each other's attention to related information. We liked to challenge each other."

Bill's life didn't revolve solely around computing, however. In the summer of 1972, before his senior year, he worked as a congressional page in Washington, D.C. By this time, Bill the shy young man had grown confident. He had starred in three school plays. He aggressively played chess and a Japanese game of strategy called Go. He drove his family's red Mustang convertible, water-skied, and went to the senior prom. He also grew closer to his mother, with whom he had frequently argued.

As to life after high school, Bill knew he had lots of options. He had good grades and test scores. On the SAT, he scored 800 (a perfect score) on the math portion and 700 on the verbal portion. He won a National Merit Scholarship. After making a quick tour of East Coast colleges, Bill applied to Harvard, Yale, and Princeton. He was accepted at all three and chose to attend Harvard.

This original Pong game was on display at the Liberty Science Center in Jersey City, New Jersey.

Chapter TWO

SPREADING HIS WINGS

HARVARD UNIVERSITY, LOCATED IN CAMBRIDGE, Massachusetts, near Boston, provided the intense intellectual experience eighteen-year-old Bill Gates craved. During his freshman year, in 1973, he studied advanced math, Greek literature, English, social science, and organic chemistry. He often skipped the classes in which he was enrolled and attended other classes just for fun. He used the university's computers and continued working on his Traf-O-Data project.

At hamburger joints, Bill discovered the video game Pong and became an avid player. With other math students, he engaged in heated discussions on many topics. When Bill predicted that one day average people would own their own computers, other Harvard math students scoffed. They couldn't envision anything less grandiose than the mainframe computers at the university's computer center.

Attending Harvard, Bill learned that he was no longer the smartest student in math class. The experience humbled Bill, who had planned to major in math. Instead, he considered majoring in law or one of the sciences. He also considered taking time off from college and getting a job. He interviewed with several companies.

During his sophomore year, Bill met a math and science student named Steve Ballmer, who lived in the same residence hall. The outgoing and charming Ballmer made sure that Bill had a life outside of his studies. The friends played the video game Breakout and attended all-night poker games in the dormitory. "He'd play poker until six in the morning, then I'd run into him at breakfast and discuss applied mathematics," Ballmer recalled. Together Gates and Ballmer took graduate-level courses in math and economics.

Meanwhile, Paul Allen had accepted a job near Boston, and he and Bill stayed close friends. Realizing that their traffic analyzing machine was not going to make it to market, they decided to focus on computer programs instead of hardware, the physical parts of computers. They talked for many hours about possible software projects. They also kept up on the computer industry's latest developments in computer-chip technology.

The January 1975 issue of *Popular Electronics* featured an article on the Altair 8800, the first personal computer—a small computer that fit on a desk—for sale to the public. The computer didn't look like much, just a rectangular box with several rows of little lights and several more rows of tiny toggle switches across the front. It had no keyboard, no disk drive—none of the parts that would later become standard on personal computers. And the buyer had to assemble the Altair 8800 from a kit. Only people who were very interested in electronics bought this early machine.

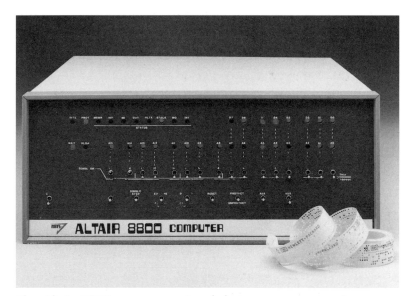

The Altair 8800 computer printed data on punch tape, bottom right.

No matter how primitive it was, the Altair 8800 was a computer, and it needed software. Gates and Allen decided to write a program that would enable the Altair to run other programs such as BASIC. They hoped to sell the program to the Altair's manufacturer, Micro Instrumentation and Telemetry System (MITS), in Albuquerque, New Mexico.

For six weeks, Bill almost lived at the Harvard computer center—that is, when he wasn't at class, grabbing a meal, or playing poker. He could nap almost anywhere and did, even in a corner of the computer lab or slumped over a keyboard. Allen came to the center when he was off work. As they neared the end of the project, Gates and Allen hired several other Harvard students to write small portions of their BASIC program. As the two had hoped, Ed Roberts, the creator of the Altair, agreed to buy the rights to use the program, called MS-BASIC, in his computers. Afterward, Gates and Allen still had to fix dozens of bugs in the program.

In the spring of 1975, as Bill finished his classes at Harvard, he debated whether or not to return in the fall. Paul Allen had accepted a job with MITS as its director of software. Bill realized that he was poised at a pivotal point in a technological revolution.

FOUNDING MICROSOFT

For decades, people at businesses, schools, laboratories, and in government had used adding machines to

Microsoft had its first offices in this Albuquerque, New Mexico, office building from September 1976 to December 1978.

calculate sums from handwritten ledgers. They had typed documents, including whole books, page by page on typewriters. If a typist needed more than one copy of a document, he or she placed carbon paper between sheets of typing paper. Making changes and correcting errors were time consuming and expensive.

Bill could see that with a personal computer calculating, typing, making multiple copies, and other business and school tasks would be easier. Bill wanted to help solve millions of people's everyday problems and make money in the process.

He decided to take a leave of absence from Harvard to start a software company with Paul Allen. Bill's parents did not agree with his decision and tried to talk him out of it. Though Bill did go back to Harvard for a semester or two, in the end, his software business won out.

In 1977 Bill Gates left Harvard for Albuquerque on what became a permanent leave of absence. Paul Allen had quit MITS in 1976. He and Bill formed a legal partnership and registered the name Microsoft with the state of New Mexico. They were in business.

But what kind of business could thrive in a hacker climate? Back then, computer hackers were people so interested in computers that they would give away their own programs for free. And they were not above copying other people's programs. Bill had caused a stir in 1975 when he wrote a letter in the *Computer Notes* newsletter. He said that computer users were stealing if they copied rather than bought computer programs. Bill argued that software programs were "intellectual property," meaning that they should be legally protected through copyrights, like books. Because of Bill's efforts, copying computer programs became illegal.

Soon companies like Apple, Commodore, and Radio Shack got into the personal computer business. As computer makers developed more powerful chips, software programs became more powerful too. The new programs could perform more complicated operations. Word-processing programs, for example, allowed users to move words and paragraphs around in typed documents. They could produce different styles and sizes of type. Other programs could show and manipulate graphic images. And the programs could perform all of these tasks faster than ever before.

Although Gates and Allen had sold the rights to MS-BASIC to MITS, they were able to get the rights back legally, without payment. At Microsoft they wrote BASIC programs to run the various new computers on the market. Each brand of computer was just different enough from the others that it needed its own customized BASIC program.

Microsoft sold its BASIC program for a very low price. Bill believed that so many people would eventually buy the program that the company would make a profit, even with the low price. Microsoft's motto was "A computer on every desk and in every home."

Though Bill could probably have gotten money from his family to help start his business, he didn't want it. He wanted Microsoft to support itself from the beginning. For three years, he worked long hours, often sixteen-hour days. He wrote computer code and handled the business end of the company. He made sales calls to companies like General Electric, National Cash Register, and Citibank. These big companies needed software for their mainframes and other computers. He also talked with computer makers about selling MS-BASIC and other programming languages with their machines.

Though he was now in his early twenties, Bill's slight

build, unruly hair, and freckles made him look like a teenager. His youthful looks sometimes gave potential buyers pause. But as soon as buyers heard him talk about his company's products, they could tell that he knew the business. As Microsoft sold more programs, Bill hired more employees. Many were old friends from Lakeside School.

When the new employees arrived at work, they found a place that was more like a college than a business. There was no dress code—programmers wore jeans. They hung posters on the walls and listened to rock music if they wanted. The company gave out free sodas. Some programmers arrived in the afternoon and worked until evening. Then they grabbed a bite to eat, maybe went to a movie, and came back to work a late-night session. They straggled home in the early morning hours, returning to work again around noon.

Despite the relaxed atmosphere, the programmers took their jobs seriously—as though they were on a mission. They were going to change the world. But exactly how much, and in what ways, wouldn't become clear until some years later.

No one at Microsoft worked harder than Bill Gates. He was so preoccupied with his work that he often forgot to tend to his appearance or eat meals. Sometimes, when his secretary came to work in the morning, she found her boss asleep on the floor of his office.

Even though he worked very hard, Bill needed to relax too. He went to movies. He bought a used sports car and took high-speed nighttime drives in the desert around Albuquerque. He racked up speeding tickets.

Bill, right, *and Paul Allen,* left, *show off some of their first software disks. The disks are sitting on the computer's keyboard.*

At least once, Paul Allen had to bail him out of jail when he forgot his driver's license.

Microsoft no longer had ties to MITS, and it was often difficult to convince programmers to move to Albuquerque, which was far from most major universities and big cities. So, in 1978, Bill decided to move the company, which then numbered a dozen employees. Although most computer companies were located in California, Gates's ties to his family were strong. He opted to move Microsoft to Bellevue, Washington, near Seattle.

Bill knew that to be truly successful, Microsoft needed to sell more than just language products like BASIC. It needed to sell word-processing and operating system software. Bill believed that personal computers would become essential for businesses. He predicted that many people would want a computer at home.

Bill also realized that Microsoft needed more efficient business practices. Bill knew that his college friend Steve Ballmer, with his business experience and social skills, would be a great asset, even though he knew little about computers. As it turned out, Ballmer was available. He became Bill's assistant and one of the company's best promoters.

DEALING WITH IBM

In 1980 IBM (International Business Machines), then the leading manufacturer of mainframe computers, decided to get into the personal computer business. Because IBM executives wanted a product ready for sale in a short time, they decided not to build their own computer from scratch. Instead, they would build a computer using parts that were already being made by other manufacturers. And instead of writing their own software for the IBM personal computer (PC), they contacted Microsoft.

Twenty-five-year-old Bill Gates agreed to provide IBM with a group of software programs, including a disk operating system. The operating system, or OS, is the master program that runs the computer. It controls the keyboard, monitor, and information storage system.

To get a head start on writing an operating system for IBM, Bill bought one from Seattle Computer Products. For a year, nearly half of the sixty employees at Microsoft worked day and night on the IBM project. They adapted the OS for the IBM machine and named it MS-DOS.

Bill licensed the system to IBM on a royalty basis, meaning that for each copy of MS-DOS sold, IBM would pay a percentage of the money to Microsoft. When IBM introduced its personal computer in 1981, buyers snapped it up. Royalties from IBM began to pour into Microsoft.

Because IBM had used off-the-shelf parts to build its PC, other computer makers could build similar computers, which came to be called "clones." The clones

Paul Allen, just before he left Microsoft in 1983

needed software too, and Bill was right there, offering MS-DOS and other products. Royalties began to pour in from PC makers everywhere. Eventually MS-DOS became the standard operating system for IBM PCs and clones (only Apple brand computers used their own operating system). All the computer users who were using MS-DOS could share files and documents.

By the end of 1982, Microsoft had sold $32 million in software. It had about two hundred employees, but it soon lost a very important one. Paul Allen learned that he had Hodgkin's disease, a treatable form of cancer, and left Microsoft in early 1983 to focus on other goals—playing in a rock band was one of them.

Though Bill felt his friend's absence, he had a company to run. Microsoft depended on him for leadership—to decide what products to make and how to sell them. The stress kept Bill up at night with insomnia.

One of the most important companies in the early computer industry was Apple, which made a popular computer called the Macintosh. To make its computers easy to use, Apple incorporated a system called the graphical user interface, or GUI (pronounced GOO-ee), which had originally been developed in the 1960s. This system also used a mouse, a device invented by Doug Engelbart at the Stanford Research Institute in 1963. By moving the mouse, Macintosh users could point to small pictures on the screen to control their computers. They didn't have to remember complicated commands. Bill could see that making computers easier to use was an important step. He believed that GUI was the key.

Microsoft Windows 1.0 was launched in November 1983.

Chapter **THREE**

BETTING ON WINDOWS

DURING THE **1980**s, **B**ILL FOCUSED **M**ICROSOFT
on two areas: developing products for individual computer users and creating an international sales force.
He added a customer service department. Microsoft
grew dramatically.

In 1982 Microsoft introduced a spreadsheet program
called Multiplan. It allowed businesspeople to perform
accounting and other financial calculations. The next
year, Microsoft came out with Word, a word-processing program featuring WYSIWYG, (pronounced
"wizzy-wig"), which stands for "What You See Is What
You Get." WYSIWYG showed words on the screen exactly as they would appear on paper, whether printed
in italics, boldface, or another typestyle.

This was the first logo for the Multiplan spreadsheet software.

Although Bill had decided to focus on software, he made a few exceptions. He ordered the creation of a piece of hardware, a mouse that would be used with an upcoming GUI program. He formed Microsoft Press, which published books about how to use Microsoft programs. He opened offices and licensed other companies to sell Microsoft products in Japan, Europe, and Australia.

Microsoft continued its relationship with IBM, licensing MS-DOS for IBM's new, powerful IBM PC-AT. In a joint venture, programmers at the two companies began to develop a more advanced operating system, OS/2. But each development team had a different idea of what the end product should include and how it should work. Eventually IBM went on to finish OS/2 by itself, leaving out many facets that Microsoft had brought to the project.

Instead of OS/2, Bill Gates bet the future of his company on an operating system he called Windows. Windows, named for the separate frames users could create on the computer screen, would feature the graphical user interface (the mouse). Instead of memorizing commands, users would operate the computer with a mouse, pointing and clicking on small pictures called icons. Windows would be user friendly. It would let people run more than one program at a time—a process called multitasking—and it would let them easily move information from one program to another.

Bill had big plans for Windows. He spent hours considering what the program would look like and how it would work. Should the windows overlap or appear next to each other? What should the icons look like? What colors should the borders, titles, and all the other visual elements on the screen be?

The thirty programmers who worked on the first version of Windows thrived on the challenge of creating an exciting new product. They often worked extremely long hours, sometimes to the point of exhaustion, to meet deadlines.

By 1984 Windows was way behind schedule. Bill often asked programmers to make changes in the program, sometimes requiring them to throw out weeks' worth of computer code and start over. This atmosphere could be frustrating for programmers and stressful for managers, several of whom left the company, "unable to tolerate the screaming fits [Bill] and Ballmer threw." According to Ballmer, Bill even threatened to fire him over the delays, although Bill later called the threat a joke.

Like the programmers, Bill maintained a hectic work schedule. Along with Steve Ballmer, he was the head salesperson for Microsoft products. And he liked to know what was going on in all areas of Microsoft—and have his say about it.

Bill didn't have much time for life outside of work. In 1983 he bought a house in his parents' neighborhood. The house had an indoor swimming pool but little furniture. The den contained a desk cluttered with computer magazines and a computer. An e-mail system allowed Microsoft employees to send messages to each other's computers at work. Since Bill's home computer was tied into the system via phone lines, he could send messages to his employees from home. And he did—sometimes in the middle of the night.

Despite all the work, Bill made a point to see his family on a regular basis. He sometimes had friends over for parties or to swim in his indoor pool. For a long time, Bill had no television—he was afraid it would distract him from his work. Finally, a friend gave him a television that was adjusted to play only videos.

As male coworkers got married, Bill threw bachelor parties. He himself had several girlfriends. For a year he dated Jill Bennett, a sales representative from another computer company. Bill and Jill shared an interest in computers and tennis and had some friends in common. What they didn't have enough of, though,

Ann Winblad, also a software engineer, dated Bill for three years beginning in 1984.

was time. Bill boasted of his seven-hour turnaround time, meaning he was back at the office only seven hours after leaving for the day. He felt dating took too much time and energy.

Another girlfriend was software entrepreneur and investor Ann Winblad, whom Bill met at a computer conference in 1984. They dated on and off for three years. They studied physics together and went on educational vacations to places like South America and Africa. While visiting the rain forests of Brazil, they studied biotechnology. In Africa they learned about evolution from a famous anthropologist. "To Bill, life is school," Ann explained. "There's always something more to learn." A slender person, Ann even persuaded fast-food junkie Bill to give up his favorite food— cheeseburgers—for a time. Ann, several years older than Bill, was ready to settle down. But Bill wasn't ready for marriage. After he and Ann stopped dating, they remained friends.

In 1985 Bill celebrated his thirtieth birthday with a roller-skating party for family, friends, and coworkers. This year also marked the tenth anniversary of Microsoft. For a decade, Bill had focused intensely on his business. His dedication was paying off. In 1985 the company sold $140 million in products, including operating systems, business software, hardware, and how-to books.

Even better, the first version of Windows had been sold in the United States that year. Windows had a few bugs, and other computer companies hadn't yet written many programs to run with it. Some computer industry specialists wondered if Windows' GUI system was really the future of personal computing. But for Bill Gates, Windows was only the beginning.

He had never imagined that his company would grow so big so fast. In fact, he had wanted to keep the staff at about one thousand employees. Yet Microsoft continued to grow, with MS-DOS bringing in steady income. The company grew so fast that Bill no longer knew the names of all his employees.

The X-shaped buildings in the foreground were the first to be built on Microsoft's Redmond, Washington, site.

As such a powerful company, Microsoft has been accused of "borrowing" ideas for programs from smaller companies in ways that are, while not necessarily illegal, at least perceived as unfair. According to such accusations, Microsoft and a company would discuss a partnership, in which the small firm would benefit from Microsoft's size and influence, while Microsoft would benefit from collaborating on a project already in development. Several of these companies, such as Micrografx and Go, have claimed that Microsoft looked at their ideas and then chose to end the partnership, later releasing similar, competing products. Bill has denied all charges of "pilfering," or stealing, saying that Microsoft simply builds upon the technology that

THE GAMES GATES PLAYS

Since he was a child, Bill Gates has been an avid game player. Even as an adult he plays games—both on and off the computer. He enjoys chess, Go, and bridge. He has studied with a bridge coach, and he belongs to an on-line bridge club, through which players log on and play with others over the Internet.

Gates likes to play tennis, and after becoming a successful businessman, he took up a game that other businesspeople often play—golf. He admits that he may never be a great golfer, but that did not stop him from playing with President Bill Clinton.

already exists. No legal action was taken at the time.

In 1986 Microsoft moved its corporate headquarters to the outskirts of Redmond, Washington, constructing four X-shaped buildings in an industrial park. In the middle of these buildings was an artificial lake that soon became known as "Lake Bill." Every employee had an office with a computer, a high-quality chair, and a nice woodsy view. Nearby canteens offered free beverages. Candy and other snacks were available at a low cost. If the weather cooperated, workers grabbed food from the cafeteria and headed for spots on the lawn. There, people played musical instruments, juggled, rode unicycles, and played basketball, soccer, and softball.

As the company roster expanded from one thousand to more than twenty thousand employees, Microsoft constructed more buildings. Its facilities eventually took up the whole office park. Yet one thing remained basically the same—the flat corporate structure. "Flat" meant that there were just enough managers to keep the programmers, marketing staff, and customer service specialists moving along at their jobs. With e-mail, employees could quickly send memos to many people at once, so the company needed few secretaries. Staff could, and did, e-mail Bill directly with their ideas, questions, and gripes.

During Microsoft's first decade, Bill gave many employees stock options—shares of the company that represented part ownership. As long as Microsoft was privately owned, employees could not sell their shares. In 1986 Microsoft "went public," selling shares on the stock exchange to institutions and people who were not employees. As a publicly owned company, Microsoft could sell stock at whatever price people were willing to pay.

Some businesses sell shares of stock to generate money for expansion. But Microsoft did not need to generate money. It had no debt and had made a profit of $30 million during the first six months of 1985. Yet Bill did need to keep his hardworking employees happy. The morning that Microsoft stock first went on sale, it sold at $21 per share. By the end of that day, the price had risen to $28 per share. Microsoft employees who had been given stock options year after year could trade their stock for cash or keep it in case the price went higher, which it did.

As the stock became more valuable, some people, including Bill Gates and Steve Ballmer, became instant millionaires—at least on paper. If they wanted cash, they'd have to sell their shares of stock. Bill sold over $1 million worth of stock, but he still owned more Microsoft stock than any other employee—forty-five percent of all the shares.

Becoming a millionaire did not change Bill much. He agonized over buying a speedboat. Although he did take a four-day sailing trip in Australia to celebrate the success of the stock offering, he returned to work with the same drive as always. He traveled cheaply on business trips. He drove his own car instead of hiring a limousine. He carried his own baggage at airports. And he still ordered his favorite cheeseburgers at fast-food restaurants.

Bill worried that employees might become distracted by watching Microsoft's stock price on the stock market. He didn't want employees daydreaming about elaborate houses, fancy cars, or other luxuries that they might buy as their stock rose in value. He also feared that some of his best employees might retire after becoming millionaires. Yet, to his pleasant surprise, most employees—even the hundreds of newly made millionaires—continued to come to work every day.

PLAYING GAMES

Bill's grandmother died in 1987. In her honor, Bill bought three and a half acres on the Hood Canal and built a retreat, dubbed "Cheerio," for family gatherings. The property included three vacation homes, tennis courts, and a spa. He also built a large structure that could be used as a business retreat. "The idea was really a tribute to [Gam], being that she was the glue that kept our family together. And that we wanted to preserve that very special opportunity for us to find times to be together even though everyone's life was moving off in different directions," Mary Gates explained.

The retreat became the site of the Microgames, a

festival for friends, family, and Microsoft employees, started in 1986. At the Microgames, the Gates clan acted as organizers and judges. The guests were to have all the fun. Divided into teams, they solved puzzles, sang, raced, and went on treasure hunts. Each year, the games had a different theme. One year guests found themselves on an African safari, another year in the Wild West.

At the 1987 Microgames, Bill met Melinda French, a new Microsoft employee. Bill was immediately attracted to the smart, witty, and independent Melinda. She had grown up in Dallas, Texas, with two brothers and a sister. Like her father, an aerospace engineer, Melinda found math exciting. She had studied computer science at Duke University in Durham, North Carolina, earning her undergraduate degree in only three years. She then earned a master's degree from Duke's business school, where a Microsoft recruiting team recognized her talent. After a round of interviews at the Redmond offices, French joined Microsoft. Upon meeting at the Microgames, she and Bill began dating.

Microsoft continued to bring new products to the marketplace. In 1987 it introduced its second version of Windows and its Excel spreadsheet software. The following year, the company's manufacturing and distribution center moved to a larger facility in Bothell, Washington. A new product support center answered more than one million customer calls each month.

On the same day in 1986 that Microsoft had moved into its headquarters in Redmond, it held its first conference on CD-ROMs (compact discs with read-only memory). CD-ROMs looked like the next hot product. They were multimedia CDs that could hold far more data than existing computer diskettes. In 1987 Microsoft sold its first CD-ROM, Microsoft Bookshelf, a single CD that held ten popular and useful reference

Melinda French had a lot in common with Bill when they met in 1987.

Bill looks through the photo archives of his newly founded company, Corbis.

books. When computer manufacturers made CD-ROM readers common on their new computers, Microsoft was ready.

With his company firmly established in Redmond, Bill decided it was time to think about building a house for himself. In 1988 and 1989, he bought parcels of land in Medina, a city on the shores of Lake Washington, two miles across the lake from his parents' home. He didn't like the house that already stood on the property, so he sold it and had it hauled away by barge.

Bill continued to think ahead. Knowing that graphic designers and publishers would soon be working with digital images—pictures that are scanned and stored by computers—he founded a company called Corbis. Corbis bought more than twenty million works of art and photography, including the famous Bettmann Archive of photographs.

The Corbis collection is stored in an on-line database. It holds pictures in many subject areas: fine arts, history, people, cultures, entertainment, science, technology, and nature. For a fee, publishers can use these images in books, magazines, newspapers, or on-line publications. Corbis can also print posters for buyers or take them on computerized trips around the world.

As the Microsoft company grew, so did Bill's wealth and celebrity status.

Chapter **FOUR**

RIDING THE WAVE

ON MAY 22, 1990, BILL GATES PUSHED HIS glasses up his nose, grinned, and walked onstage at Center City in New York City. He was there to launch Windows 3.0—the third version of Windows. In the audience and via television, thousands of reporters and computer employees watched the presentation. Industry leaders praised the new Windows. A short, MTV-style video hyped the program and kicked off a six-month advertising campaign. Microsoft had spent $3 million on the launch day alone and more than $10 million total to make Windows 3.0 the fastest-moving software product in the country.

In the first two weeks after its release, buyers snapped up more than one hundred thousand copies of Windows 3.0. By the end of 1991, Microsoft had shipped 4 million copies in 12 languages to 24 countries. As part of the Windows Ready-to-Run program, computer manufacturers were now including Windows as standard software on their computers. Even the Microsoft mouse was swept up in the surge—buyers trapped 6 million. Bill finally had a software best-seller.

During this time, he continued to think about his dream house. To find a plan he liked, he hired an architect to run an international design competition. The winner was a house to be made of concrete, steel, wood, and stone. It would not overpower the site. It would nestle into a hillside, with lots of windows to offer lake and mountain views. "I wanted craftsmanship but nothing ostentatious," explained Bill.

Also on Bill's mind were investments outside of Microsoft. As a child, he had dreamed about becoming a scientist. He had long been interested in biotechnology, evolution, the brain, and DNA. "I'm sometimes asked what field I would have chosen if not computers," Bill said. "It's hard to say for sure, but I've always been fascinated by biology and genetics."

Biotechnology involves using technology to make biological discoveries and products. In 1990 three scientists who had already made important medical discoveries invited Bill to invest in their new biotechnology company, ICOS, and to join its board of directors. Bill studied the scientists' prospectus and invested $5 million.

ICOS was the first of several biotech companies Bill backed. Why would someone as rich as Bill Gates invest in new businesses? He didn't need to make more money. Instead, Bill wanted to use his money to advance technology and help people.

In October 1991, Bill gave $12 million to create a department of molecular biology at the University of Washington. With this new department, the university was able to convince a famous geneticist, Leroy Hood, to do research there. Hood is a leader in mapping genes in the human body. His work might lead to cures for fatal diseases. Before making his donation, Bill had studied Hood's research on DNA and had met with him.

A few months earlier, in July 1991, Mary Gates had called her son and said that she wanted him to meet another famous person—billionaire investor Warren Buffett. Though Bill said he was very busy, he and Melinda flew by helicopter to Cheerio, the family summer home, where Buffett and other guests had gathered. Immediately, Gates and Buffett hit it off. They found they had much in common, including a keen mind for business, a sense of humor, and a fondness for hamburgers. At Buffett's suggestion, Bill again took up playing bridge. At Bill's suggestion, the non-computer-savvy Buffett joined an on-line bridge club and became a computer user. Buffett called Bill's business sense extraordinary. "If Bill had started a hot dog stand, he would have become the hot dog king of the world," Buffett declared.

In September 1997, Bill's estate was still not complete.

Though Windows 3.0 was a best-seller, Bill didn't rest. By 1992 programmers had improved Windows in a thousand ways. Bill knew that if he didn't keep improving a product greatly, no one would want to buy new versions—they would just keep using the old one. Microsoft continued to improve not only Windows but also its other programs. For example, the company offered its Word 2.0 word-processing program in twenty-two different languages.

While Bill worked to improve Microsoft products, builders began excavating the site for his dream home. Because Seattle is located in an earthquake zone, the design required tons of concrete and many beams and supports. For beams, builders recycled Douglas fir timbers from a lumber mill that was being torn down.

Inside the house, a master computer would run the lights, temperature controls, security system, and other features. Flat LCDs (liquid-crystal displays) on the walls would be programmed to show different pieces of artwork. Explained Bill, "I wanted a house that would accommodate sophisticated, changing technology, but in an unobtrusive way that made it clear that technology was the servant, not the master."

The builders worked first on the guest house, so they could use it to test another new technology. High-bandwidth wiring would allow the computers running the house to be superfast.

LEARNING TO LOVE

With her combination of intelligence and people skills, Melinda French rose quickly through the ranks at Microsoft. By 1993 she was the product unit manager for Microsoft Publisher, a desktop publishing system. She supervised the work of some forty employees.

Since meeting at the Microgames in 1987, Bill and Melinda had dated on and off. On business trips, Bill sometimes went out with other women, but when he was in town, he gravitated toward Melinda. The couple went to dinner, movies, and plays. Once they took a trip to Australia. It became obvious to people who knew Bill well that he and Melinda had something special.

Bill and Melinda attend a Seattle SuperSonics basketball game in Seattle.

Bill's parents were concerned about him. He seemed to be too busy with work to have time for love. So after Bill and Melinda had been dating for some time, Bill's mother asked him when he was going to give Melinda an engagement ring. Finally, on March 20, 1993, Bill surprised Melinda. On a chartered flight from Palm Springs, California, to Seattle, Bill arranged for a detour to Omaha, Nebraska.

There, Warren Buffett met the couple. Buffett had arranged for a famous jewelry store to be opened for them alone. The couple picked out a diamond engagement ring.

Two days later, the public relations department at Microsoft announced the engagement. The news made headlines around the world. Many people who knew Bill and Melinda thought they were well matched. "She's really a wonderful person, the perfect match for him," said Bill Gates Sr. "Very, very bright, very organized, very supportive, very interested in family and good family life."

Melinda could give Bill personal happiness and could understand his business, which was such an important part of his life. Yet she was concerned that by marrying the richest man in the world, she would lose her privacy. She did not want to be fodder for the newspapers. So she contacted relatives, friends, and former neighbors and teachers. She asked them not to talk about her to reporters. She was also concerned for her safety—being so wealthy could make her a target for kidnappers.

Since she and Bill were going to live together, Melinda wanted some changes made to the house under construction. She didn't care for the exposed beams and rough concrete. She wanted her own study and a dressing room. She wanted a kitchen that would suit a family instead of just a noncooking bachelor. And she wanted security people for protection and privacy.

Finally, Melinda knew she would have to leave her

Bill and Melinda live a high-profile life. Here, they are going to a Planet Hollywood restaurant opening.

job at Microsoft. Even before the marriage actually took place, the people Melinda had been supervising became uncomfortable with her personal connection to the company's owner. Instead of working at Microsoft, Melinda would sit on boards of directors of other companies and work for charitable organizations.

On the business front, Bill was taking Microsoft full speed into multimedia products. In 1993 Microsoft began to sell more CD-ROM titles. These included Microsoft Encarta, the first multimedia encyclopedia designed for a computer. With sound, animation, illustrations, graphs, maps, and photographs, Encarta brought subjects to life. Later, Microsoft sold other

CDs, some of which focused on specific subjects such as dinosaurs, movies, music, baseball, and golf.

For the business world, Microsoft brought out its high-powered Windows NT (New Technology) operating system. With this software, businesspeople could run a whole network of computer terminals from a single PC. They could keep track of how many products they had in storage. They could keep track of sales and how much money their company earned. They could do complicated calculations. *PC Magazine* gave Windows NT an award for technical excellence.

Melinda has become involved in many charities. She served as the keynote speaker at the ninetieth anniversary of Children's Hospital in Seattle.

Chapter **FIVE**

GETTING A LIFE

BILL AND MELINDA MADE ARRANGEMENTS TO marry on January 1, 1994, on the island of Lanai in Hawaii. They chose the island because it is privately owned and they could control who would attend the wedding. No party crashers were allowed, especially uninvited photographers. Just 130 invited guests would be there.

Though they tried to keep the date and place a secret, word leaked out. The story made the newspapers. But security people turned away reporters who tried to get to the island.

Bill paid for the guests, many of them rich and famous themselves, to stay at a hotel on the island. The day before the wedding, the male guests played golf and ate lunch with the groom. The female guests attended a luncheon for the bride. That night, Bill and Melinda treated guests to a luau (a Hawaiian outdoor party). As a surprise for his wife-to-be, Bill arranged for her favorite singer, Willie Nelson, to perform. Melinda was delighted. Everyone danced on the beach. The evening ended with a dazzling fireworks show.

On their wedding day, Melinda wore a white silk-faced organza wedding gown strewn with pearls. Five bridesmaids in pink gowns attended her. Bill wore a white dinner jacket and black trousers. Steve Ballmer was his best man.

On a cliff high above the Pacific Ocean, at the twelfth tee of a golf course, Bill and Melinda exchanged vows. Melinda, a devout Catholic, wanted a religious wedding. At the end of the short Roman Catholic ceremony, Bill slipped a wedding ring on Melinda's finger. They kissed as the setting sun cast a pink glow over the sky. "We're both extremely happy and looking forward to a long, wonderful life together," Bill later announced to the public.

Yet in life, joy and sorrow often intermingle, and for Bill Gates fate did not make an exception. Shortly before he and Melinda married, Bill learned that his mother was battling breast cancer. Though she had the best care possible, the cancer overtook her within a year. In the early morning of June 10, 1994, Mary Gates died.

Bill and his mother had been very close, and her

Although no reporters were allowed on the island, some photographers managed to take wedding photographs by boat. Bill and Melinda are to the left, facing the edge of the cliff.

death hit him hard. When he heard the news, he got in his car and rushed to his parents' house. On the way, a police officer pulled him over for speeding. The officer recognized Bill and, seeing tears streaming down his face, asked what had happened. A choked-up Bill explained that his mother had just died. The officer waved Bill on, gently admonishing him to drive a little slower.

Several days later, Bill spoke at his mother's memorial service, which was packed with family, friends, and colleagues. Then he turned to his family and work for solace. Melinda helped see him through the difficult months that followed.

LIVING AS A CELEBRITY

The Federal Trade Commission (FTC) is a government agency that keeps watch over large and successful companies, to make sure they conduct their business legally. In 1991 the FTC and the U.S. Department of Justice began to investigate Microsoft. In 1994 Justice Department lawyers sued Microsoft over its sales practices.

Microsoft had always insisted that computer makers who sold the Microsoft operating system had to sell other Microsoft products as well. The lawsuit put an end to this practice, which was considered illegal. Even so, Bill Gates did not admit that his company had done anything wrong.

As the value of Microsoft stock continued to rise, Bill became a billionaire, passing Warren Buffett to top the list of America's richest people. With $525,000 a year in salary and bonuses, Bill was actually not the highest-paid employee at Microsoft. But he sold shares in the company at regular intervals, using money from the sales to pay his taxes, build his home, and invest in other businesses.

Bill didn't show off his wealth. He tried to keep a low profile. To reporters, Bill Gates was a commodity. He was a celebrity, and he couldn't avoid the media. But Bill thought that talking to reporters was a waste of time. He was impatient with what he called "stupid questions," and he earned a reputation for rudeness. When one television reporter stated that competing with Microsoft was like being in a knife fight, Bill lost his temper and walked off the stage.

Some critics focused on Bill's wealth, calculating that he earned about $150 each second. At that pay rate, they figured, it wouldn't be worthwhile for Bill to pick a $500 bill off the sidewalk. He could earn more money just by walking on. When he donated millions of dollars to charity, people openly questioned his motives or criticized the amount or timing of the donation. For example, when the Gates Library Foundation began donating computers to libraries,

Bill and Melinda look on as children use computers during an event hosted by the Gates Library Foundation.

some detractors suggested that Bill just wanted to sell more software to the libraries. Other critics simply said that he hadn't donated enough.

INVESTING IN THE FUTURE

Calling himself a "steward of a share of society's resources," in 1994 Bill announced plans to return his money to society in positive ways. "Giving away money effectively is almost as hard as earning it in the first place," he once said. That year, he and Melinda created the William H. Gates Foundation, which would funnel money to worthy projects. Bill's father, William H. Gates Sr., retired from his law firm to run the foundation.

The foundation focused on four areas: education, worldwide public health and population issues, non-

Dr. Effie Petersdorf, left, *and Dr. John A. Hansen,* right, *go over some work at the Fred Hutchinson Cancer Research Center.*

profit civic and arts organizations, and campaigns to create endowments (like scholarships) in the Puget Sound area. Bill and Melinda also donated $1 million to the Fred Hutchinson Cancer Research Center in Seattle.

In recalling his school years, Bill said: "Letting students use a computer in the late 1960s was a pretty amazing choice at the time in Seattle—and one I'll always be grateful for." Paul Allen, recovered from his illness, had stayed with Microsoft as a member of its board of directors. Bill and Paul showed their gratitude by paying for a new science building at Lakeside School. The two friends flipped a coin to decide whose name would go first on the building. Inside Allen-Gates Hall, they named the auditorium in memory of their classmate Kent Evans. Along with Steve Ballmer, Bill also paid for a new computer center for Harvard University. The price tag: $15 million from Bill, $10 million from Ballmer.

In 1994 Bill joined Craig McCaw, a pioneer in the world of cellular telephones, in an ambitious venture. They created a company called Teledesic. Its goal was to circle the earth with 288 low-orbiting satellites that would provide two-way communications for the entire world. Each of the satellites would cost nearly $20 million to build, so Teledesic needed many investors. "I am investing in Teledesic because I believe it is a very exciting idea with the potential to truly connect the world together in a way it never has been before,"

Bill said. If the satellite network succeeds, information could travel from earth to satellite and back at speeds as fast as through fiber-optic cables. The network would give people in areas without basic telephone service the ability to communicate using handheld devices.

Some investments were more personal. In 1994 the *Codex Leicester*, a scientific notebook written by Leonardo da Vinci, was put up for sale. In the eighteen-page notebook, Leonardo wrote about many subjects: astronomy, geology, paleontology, and hydraulics. A fan of Leonardo since boyhood, Bill paid $30.8 million for the unique masterpiece. "Leonardo was one of the most amazing people who ever lived. He was a genius in more fields than any scientist of any age and an astonishing painter and sculptor," Bill explained with enthusiasm. "I bought the manuscript for personal pleasure." When not on loan to museums, the *Codex Leicester* would be housed in Bill's personal library.

CHANGING DIRECTION

Bill Gates has said that the growth of the Internet—the worldwide network of computers linked by phone lines—is the most important event since the creation of the personal computer. The Internet started as a network of government computers in the 1970s. At first only scientists and military officials used the Internet. When businesspeople discovered the system,

The monitor in the background shows a later version of Microsoft's web browser, Internet Explorer.

they wanted to use it to advertise products and services. Schools and libraries realized that the system could be used to spread information. As more organizations began posting material on the Internet, the World Wide Web was born.

As early as 1994, Microsoft added hypertext markup language (HTML) to its word-processing system. HTML is used to create web pages. But creating tools for the Internet wasn't Bill Gates's top goal in 1994. "Getting Windows 95 done was the top priority;

getting Windows NT to critical mass in the market was the top priority," Bill remembered.

Late in 1994, however, Bill realized what some of his employees had already been trying to tell him—that the Internet would be the communication tool of the future. He realized that he had better make quick changes at Microsoft. Otherwise, his company would be left in the dust of other companies that were making software for the Internet.

On May 26, 1995, Bill wrote a long e-mail memo to his employees. In "The Internet Tidal Wave," he announced, "Now I assign the Internet the highest level of importance. In this memo I want to make clear that our focus on the Internet is critical to every part of our business." Bill was energized.

He asked leaders of all the project groups in Microsoft to add Internet communication and information retrieval features to their programs. They started by adding a web browser, Internet Explorer, to the newest Windows operating system. The browser let PC users bring Internet sites to their own computer screens. Later in 1995, Bill announced his plan to supply software for networks of computers that could work together over the Internet. Microsoft would also develop software for creating websites with graphics, animation, video, and audio. It would make software for companies that put websites on the Internet. Bill described the new focus: "We are as focused on the Internet as we were on graphical computing—all of our products treat the Internet as the big opportunity."

Meanwhile, in a personal effort, Bill and Melinda made a special gift to honor Bill's mother, Mary. On the anniversary of her death, they donated $10 million to the University of Washington to establish the Mary Gates Endowment for Students. Mary had always placed a high value on education. With this scholarship, many undergraduate students would benefit.

In mid-1995, Microsoft launched Windows 95. It was a new operating system—and a whole lot more. The system included CD, fax, and modem software. More important, its overall design was simple and clean. It made complicated jobs easy to perform.

On August 24, fifteen large white tents decorated the lawn outside Microsoft headquarters in Redmond. A circuslike atmosphere prevailed. The first tent featured Bill Gates and special guest Jay Leno, host of *The Tonight Show*. The fourteen other tents held representatives from software companies demonstrating programs designed to run on Windows 95.

Bill came onstage wearing white slacks and a navy blue sport shirt bearing the Windows logo. He and Leno traded jokes. Saying that Bill wasn't so smart, Leno added that he'd once gone to Bill's home and found the VCR flashing twelve o'clock. Gesturing at Leno, Bill quipped, "Windows 95 is so easy, even a talk show host can figure it out." Then Leno introduced Windows 95 to 2,500 specially invited people—

The Tonight Show *host Jay Leno was invited to be a special guest at the kickoff event for Windows 95 software.*

500 of them journalists from more than 30 countries. They had all come to get a look at the fruit of two years of work writing 15 million lines of computer code.

As Windows 95 was coming out, Microsoft also launched its own on-line service, Microsoft Network (MSN). As with other on-line services, people could pay Microsoft a fee each month for Internet connection. Then they could use Internet features like e-mail, news services, banking services, and chat rooms. Though Windows 95 sold rapidly, not many users joined the new on-line network. But if at first it didn't succeed, Microsoft would try again. Within a year, it had redesigned MSN. People began to join the network, but not in big enough numbers to give Microsoft a profit.

With the launch of Windows 95 behind him, Bill took time off to travel. With a group of friends, including Bill Gates Sr. and Warren Buffett, Bill and Melinda took a two-week trip to China. They traveled by train and boat through the country. At the Great Wall of China, Bill tried to fly a kite, but the wind wouldn't cooperate. When not viewing the scenery or sightseeing, Bill played bridge. Melinda also organized fun activities, like karaoke singing and trivia quizzes.

In the capital city of Beijing, Bill met with Chinese leader and Communist Party president Jiang Zemin. Bill, Melinda, and Warren Buffett posed for photos with Jiang. Ever the businessman, Bill paid a quick visit to Microsoft's Beijing office. As a souvenir, he bought a nine-foot-tall clay statue of a Chinese warrior. It was a replica of a famous statue that had been unearthed by archaeologists.

Bill celebrated his fortieth birthday with a party at his new but still unfinished home. Bill had taken up golf. So for this special occasion, Melinda arranged for an eighteen-hole miniature golf course to be set up on the grounds. She and Bill dressed in old-fashioned golfing clothes, and the eighty guests came in costume too. As a birthday surprise, Melinda invited four of his female friends to come dressed as cheerleaders. Their lettered sweaters spelled out B-I-L-L.

Bill decided that it would be worthwhile to educate

the public about computers and Microsoft. He began writing a newspaper column, published by the *New York Times* syndicate and on Microsoft's website. In some columns, he answered readers' questions, such as how small businesses might use computers, what young people should study if they want a job working with computers, and what future technology might become important. In other columns, Bill wrote about the qualities that make someone a good manager, employee, or computer programmer. Readers sent questions by e-mail to <askbill@microsoft.com>.

PREDICTING THE FUTURE

In November 1995, Bill published the first edition of *The Road Ahead*. In this book with an attached CD-ROM, he described the history of computing and predicted future trends. A year later, he published a revised edition, which focused more on the Internet. Both books were best-sellers in more than twenty countries. Bill donated the $3 million he earned from the sale of *The Road Ahead* to the National Foundation for the Improvement of Education. This nonprofit organization helps teachers learn to use computers and other technology in their classrooms.

Bill explains in *The Road Ahead* that he has always tried to take the long view—meaning he looks far into the future and plans ahead. He tries to make decisions that will be good for his company over a long period, not just in the immediate future. But with technology changing so quickly, it is difficult to predict what will happen in the computer industry. For example, even Bill Gates nearly missed the Internet turnoff in the road of developing technology.

In the twenty-five years since personal computers were first made, they have been getting more and more powerful. They have more memory and can work faster. In *The Road Ahead,* Bill predicts that faster, more powerful computers will lead to more products, such as digital TV and computers the size of a wallet.

Bill and Melinda attend many charity functions together.

Chapter **SIX**

HAVING IT ALL

BILL GATES HAD COME FAR SINCE **1975,** WHEN he left Harvard to follow his dream. He had started a successful company from scratch. He had become enormously rich. He had married the love of his life. What was left for him to achieve?

When he was in his twenties and early thirties, Bill hadn't wanted to be a family man. He had dated casually, not wanting to settle down. He even said that children scared him. But after Melinda came on the scene, and after he became "Uncle Trey" to his sister's children, Bill's views gradually changed.

On April 26, 1996, Bill was at Melinda's side when she gave birth to their daughter, Jennifer Katharine Gates. Later, he made jokes to colleagues about more than business worries keeping him up at night. In his desk drawer at work, he kept a photograph of himself holding Jennifer. "I used to think I wouldn't be all that interested in the baby until she was two or so and could talk," Bill admitted. "But I'm totally into it now. She's just started to say 'ba-ba' and have a personality."

Bill's father was happy to see his son in this new role. "He just loves that little girl," said Bill Gates Sr. "It's so marvelous to see. It's very gratifying to a father to see his own son has the same feeling I had about him and his sisters. It's really gratifying."

On the business front, MSNBC, a joint project between Microsoft and the NBC television network, debuted in July 1996. The project brought news and information to television viewers via the MSNBC channel, while Internet users could get more information on the MSNBC website. They could also read an on-line magazine called *Slate*.

COMING HOME

Construction on Bill's house had dragged on for six years. Bill was aware that neighbors might be tired of having construction vehicles, noise, and dust nearby. So he hired work crews to mow the neighbors' lawns, do free landscaping, and wash the dust off their vehicles.

Although the house wasn't entirely completed in late 1997, the Gates family moved in. Five pavilions, connected by underground tunnels, make up the complex.

One pavilion holds a grand entry hall, guest rooms, a theater, a dining room that seats 120, conference rooms, a computer room, and a library. (The library is Bill's favorite room. He hired a book dealer to help stock it.) Another pavilion contains a beach house, hot tub, and swimming pool. Another holds a caretaker's home. The family's private living space takes up two floors of the main pavilion. It includes a family room, exercise room, trampoline room, and bedrooms for children and a nanny. Parking space for twenty cars, hidden underground, houses Bill's collection of sports cars. The informal landscaping, which includes wetlands and a trout stream, makes the house seem like a natural part of the environment.

The MSNBC newsroom

After waiting seven years and paying more than $54 million for the house, Bill expected everything to work. Yet he wrote in his newspaper column about one technological bug. He had a movable television screen set up at the end of his bed. One night, the screen wouldn't move down when he was done watching—it wouldn't even turn off. Instead, it glowed bright blue. Bill had to throw a blanket over it so he could go to sleep.

Bill and Melinda continued to make charitable contributions. They gave $100 million to a health organization that would vaccinate children in poor countries. They contributed $200 million to the Gates Library Foundation, organized in 1995 to help libraries in the United States and Canada take advantage of computer technology. The foundation considered the needs of libraries in low-income states and poverty-stricken urban areas and gave them computers and software. By the year 2002, Bill hopes to connect every library in every poor community to the Internet. With the Internet, someone in a poor area can use the same resources as those in well-to-do neighborhoods, Bill pointed out.

Although Bill viewed the Internet as a powerful educational resource, he still valued books. "It all goes back to the early experience that both Melinda and I had growing up with libraries in our communities," he explained. "I loved to check out books." He insisted that libraries not neglect their book collections just because they had computers. "Even though my house has a lot of technology, and this grant to libraries relates to technology, if you want to do something good for children, the most important thing you can do is cultivate a love of reading and to get them to be competent browsing through books and checking out books. I'm already doing that with my daughter," Bill said.

Although Bill tried to downplay his wealth, he was not immune to the problems, serious or laughable, that being rich could cause. In March 1997, Bill received a frightening letter. The writer, a young man named Adam Quinn Pletcher, threatened to kill Gates if he didn't pay him $5 million. FBI agents caught the man, who was also wanted for defrauding people on the Internet. About the time Pletcher went on trial, Bill was in Belgium for business. On his way to meet with Belgian officials, Bill got a surprise. Pranksters shoved two custard pies in his face. Startled but unhurt, Bill wiped his face and glasses and went on to the meeting. He later quipped, "The worst part was that the pies were not very tasty."

TESTIFYING BEFORE CONGRESS

On March 2, 1998, Bill met Melinda in Washington, D.C. Like other tourists, they visited the Capitol and the National Gallery. They grabbed a quick pizza for dinner and went back to their hotel. Bill wanted to prepare for the next day, when he would testify about the computer industry before a committee made up of members of Congress. He finished typing up notes on his laptop computer and rehearsed aloud his five-minute speech.

Bill was part of a panel of computer company leaders who spoke at the hearing. He told the story of how Microsoft had succeeded by constantly improving its products. He pointed out that competition among computer software makers was fierce and how competition kept software prices low. He emphasized that the government should not interfere in the computer business by telling software makers how to design their products. After the hearing, Bill signed autographs and talked with reporters.

Then Bill and Melinda caught a flight to New York City. Bill had been invited to help celebrate the seventy-fifth anniversary of *Time* magazine at a fancy dinner at Radio City Music Hall. At this dinner, famous guests were to give short speeches, paying tribute to important people of the twentieth century. Bill was asked to speak about the Wright Brothers, inventors of the airplane. He was a little nervous. He was used to speaking to computer specialists, not celebrities. Yet his enthusiasm for the Wright Brothers came through in his talk.

The next morning, Bill visited a school in the Harlem area of New York. There, he spoke with sixth graders who were using laptop computers as a way to improve their learning skills. Then he visited the New York Public Library for a question-and-answer session

Bill testifies before the Senate Judiciary Committee while Melinda, background center, *and Scott McNealy,* foreground right, *of Sun Microsystems listen.*

with television reporter Charlie Rose.

At the end of this unusually busy week, Bill was glad to get home to see Jennifer. She and "Dada" liked to play together, read books, and play with a Barney program on the computer. Around the Gates household, Bill had to be careful not to say the word *computer* around Jennifer. If he did, the two-year-old would follow him around, saying " 'puter, 'puter, 'puter," until he played a computer game with her. "I'm very lucky. My daughter is a very happy, joyful person," Bill said.

In July 1998, Bill gave a speech at a party at Microsoft headquarters to celebrate the launch of Windows 98. Until then, Windows programs had been designed especially for business PC users. Windows 98 was the first operating system made particularly with home PC users in mind. Bill predicted that by the year 2001, six of every ten homes in the United States would have PCs. Of those six homes, five would have computers hooked up to the Internet. "The PC and the Internet will become as fundamental tomorrow as the automobile is today," he predicted.

BATTLING IN THE COURTS

But Microsoft's future role in the computer industry was uncertain because more legal battles loomed on the horizon. The owners of some computer companies accused Microsoft of being a monopoly—a company that has nearly complete control of an industry. A monopoly can control the prices of the products it sells. It can charge unfairly high prices or sell products at such low prices that other companies, unable to match these prices, go out of business. Because nine out of ten new computers sold in 1998 had Microsoft's Windows 95 already installed, some people suggested that the company held a monopoly on personal computer operating systems.

In October 1998, the U.S. Justice Department and twenty states sued Microsoft, alleging that the company had been forcing computer makers to sell its Internet Explorer browser if they wanted a license to sell Windows 95. Lawyers for the Justice Department also tried to prove that Microsoft held a monopoly on operating systems and that this monopoly harmed consumers. Moreover, government lawyers accused Microsoft of using illegal practices to keep other makers of Internet browsers from competing. Their arguments were persuasive.

Though Bill Gates did not testify at the trial, government lawyers had questioned him on videotape beforehand. The lawyers then showed pieces of the videotape during the trial. Bill felt that by projecting the video on a large screen and showing his answers out of context, they portrayed him as a dictator and a villain. Others felt that Bill did run a monopolistic company that was out to crush all competitors. Reporters had a field day, speculating on the outcome of the trial and what it would mean for Microsoft and Bill.

The trial moved at a fast pace. In December the attorney general of South Carolina decided the case against Microsoft was weak and removed his state as a participant in the trial. After a two-week holiday recess, the trial resumed in January 1999.

Microsoft lawyers stated their case. They called witnesses who testified that Microsoft did not harm consumers with its products or policies. Instead, the witnesses argued, Microsoft offered computer users good products at reasonable prices. Witnesses also described the tough competition Microsoft faced—specifically from companies that made handheld computers and Internet software. In March U.S. District Judge Thomas Penfield Jackson, who presided over the trial, ordered a three-month recess so that he could try another case. During the break, government lawyers held talks with Microsoft lawyers, but the two sides could not come to an out-of-court agreement. The trial resumed in June 1999. With the final witness leaving the stand on the seventy-sixth day of proceedings, Judge Jackson had mountains of documents and testimony to consider before reaching a verdict.

What was Gates doing during the trial? As well as his daily work at Microsoft, he was putting the finishing touches on his new book, *Business @ the Speed of Thought*. Gates predicted that within ten years, business operations would change dramatically. Because computers make more information available to workers, the workers need to learn how to use this information to improve their companies. In his book, Gates suggested ways for business leaders to use digital information and gave examples of how some companies are doing so already.

When the book appeared in March 1999, Gates went on tour to promote it. He gave interviews and appeared on television shows. As with his earlier book, Gates donated much of his share of the money from the sale of the book to charity.

Also in March, Microsoft launched Internet Explorer

5.0, an improved version of the company's web browser. Within a week, users had downloaded one million copies of the browser from the Internet.

Privately, Bill and Melinda were awaiting the birth of their second child. When Rory John Gates was born on May 23, 1999, Bill took a short leave from Microsoft. "Bill and Melinda are thrilled to be new parents once again," a Microsoft spokesperson announced. "Jennifer is very excited to have a brother."

Although his company and his new family keep Bill busy, he does take time out for kayaking and other activities.

Chapter *SEVEN*

ROCKING THROUGH THE DAY

GONE ARE THE TIMES WHEN BILL GATES SPENDS sixteen hours a day at his office or stays up two nights in a row and crashes on his office floor for a nap. After getting married in January 1994, the boss cut his workday to twelve hours during the week. On weekends he works only eight hours each day. He even takes off some weekends to play golf or take vacations with his family.

Other software makers hoped that married life would distract Bill from his work at Microsoft. Yet Bill is as hardworking and efficient as ever. He doesn't like to waste a minute. Bill explained, "Time is the scarce resource and I treat it that way." He employs a personal assistant and uses an on-line calendar to budget his time. He also regularly reviews how he is spending his time, to see if and how he could be more efficient.

After a short commute by car from his home on Lake Washington, Bill arrives at the Microsoft campus in Redmond. From the outside, Microsoft world head-quarters looks more like a college than a business cen-ter. Its twenty-five low-rise red brick buildings are lined with windows that give a view of landscaped lawns.

On the inside, Bill works in an office much like

Lake Bill 2 on Microsoft's Redmond, Washington, campus

everyone else's. It has a desk with a chair, a sofa, and a coffee table. A few pictures—one of a Pentium computer chip, another of Leonardo da Vinci—decorate the office walls. A framed photo of automobile manufacturer Henry Ford reminds Bill that even Ford, the inventor of the assembly line and founder of one of the world's most successful companies, could fall to second place behind a rival.

What does Bill do all day? Working from two computers at the same time, Bill runs the company largely by e-mail. Every day, he gets hundreds of e-mails from Microsoft employees worldwide. He spends several hours each day sending out one hundred e-mails of his own. Each month, he meets with his top managers to go over business strategy.

Microsoft maintains a company library, and Bill uses it heavily. He reads the *Wall Street Journal,* the Sunday *New York Times,* the *Economist,* and other weekly news magazines. And, of course, he gets information from the Internet. If anything, Bill wishes he had more time each day to read.

Unlike the programmers who work directly on software, Bill is an overseer. Instead of writing computer code, he reviews the programmers' work. He asks questions and gives feedback about products. Sometimes the discussions can get pretty intense, with Bill rocking to and fro. The rocking is one of Bill's trademarks. He says the motion helps him focus his thinking.

Bill doesn't hesitate to call an idea inappropriate or a waste of time. He is famous for the phrase, "That's the dumbest idea I have ever heard." But the comment is meant to criticize the idea—not the person presenting it.

After twenty years of creating software, Bill remains enthusiastic about the process. He thrives on being with smart and creative people. Developing a new product is still the superfun process that he first experienced as a teenager programming a computer.

He spends about three-quarters of his time with product development teams. "I get a lot of pleasure out of sitting down with these groups," Bill explains. "That's why I make sure the majority of my time is spent with product groups. That's what I like, and that's where I think I can make a contribution. So the fun is still there, and software creation is still as much a mix of artistry and science as it has ever been."

How can writing software be both art and science? It's a given that programmers must have good math skills and must think logically—that's the science part. Yet visual aspects of programs—how elements will look on the computer screen—require software designers to have a sense of style. And even mathematics can be artistic—lines of computer code that do a job in the most efficient way are beautiful in Bill Gates's eyes.

Through example, Bill promotes creativity and hard

Software is tested at Microsoft's Usability Lab.

work. Some evenings, he wanders around the company buildings. He peeks in offices to see who is around. He looks at pictures that workers have put on their office walls. He tries to get a sense of how people feel about their work. He might ask one of the last-to-leave workers for opinions about company projects or the larger world of technology.

Bill believes that the employees are the core of Microsoft. Without them, Microsoft could never get products to market. The company rewards employees for their creativity and hard work with good salaries, promotions, and valuable Microsoft stock.

Bill makes hiring smart and creative people a top

priority. Although he dropped out of Harvard to found Microsoft, he insists that the company hire college graduates. Microsoft recruiting teams interview candidates at colleges nationwide to find the brightest programmers and businesspeople available.

Bill spends about a quarter of each year traveling, both in the United States and abroad. On these trips, each workday might last an exhausting sixteen hours. En route to a foreign locale, Bill reads books and magazines about the country. When he arrives, he meets with Microsoft's local representatives to discuss business strategy. He talks about Microsoft products to audiences of all kinds: government officials, business leaders, students, and the press.

He listens to the concerns and suggestions of computer users. "I never get bored," he has said of traveling abroad. "Even though 80 percent of what you hear from customers is the same all over the world, you always learn something that makes doing business in each country unique, or else something you can apply to our business elsewhere. Believe me, I've got plenty to do already, so I wouldn't come on these trips if I didn't think I was getting something out of it that really helps Microsoft sell software."

Every year, Bill and other top employees take a weeklong retreat from the office. Bill calls this time "Think Week," and that's what the participants do. They do research, think, and talk about what the future might hold. They talk about what role Microsoft might play in this future. They set priorities. "I work hard because I love my work," Bill explains. "It's not an addiction, and I like doing a lot of other things, but I find my work very exciting. . . . I often say I have the best job in the world, and I mean it."

UNCERTAINTIES AHEAD

In November 1999, Judge Jackson ruled on the Microsoft case. He declared Microsoft a monopoly whose influence hurts consumers. "Microsoft has demonstrated that it will use its prodigious market power and immense profits to harm any firm that insists on pursuing initiatives that could intensify competition against one of Microsoft's core products," the judge wrote in his findings.

The judge addressed specific cases of Microsoft's attempts to harm other companies, citing their interaction with Intel, a maker of microprocessors (chips), as one example. In 1995 Intel was working on a product that Microsoft felt would threaten Windows. Bill met with Intel CEO Andy Grove a number of times, eventually telling him that Microsoft would not support PCs run by Intel chips unless Intel stopped development of their new product. Needing Microsoft's support, Intel ended the project, and Bill later wrote an e-mail to other Microsoft executives saying, "if Intel is not sticking totally to its part of the deal let me know."

Another example of Microsoft's influence was their

agreement with Compaq, a personal computer company. Compaq had decided to sell their PCs with the web browser Netscape Navigator already installed. Microsoft offered to charge Compaq a special, very low price for Windows if they would agree to pre-install Microsoft's web browser instead. Judge Jackson stated that this example revealed "the pressure that Microsoft is willing to apply to [companies] that show reluctance to cooperate."

Bill responded to the judge's announcement by saying that this finding is only a small step in the legal process. He still plans to "win the war." In December 1999, while the media speculated about what punishment Microsoft might receive, Microsoft representatives and Justice Department lawyers met privately to broker a solution. Would Judge Jackson order Microsoft to be broken up into several smaller companies? Would he order the Windows source code to be made public? Where would the case go now, people wondered. As 1999 came to a close, Microsoft watchers were still wondering what would happen to Gates's life work.

In January 2000, Bill promoted his friend and company president, Steve Ballmer, to chief executive officer (CEO) of Microsoft. Bill said he wants to focus on developing new technologies for the future and return to shaping the company's next generation of Windows products.

Though Microsoft and Bill have faced challenges

over the years, few people would dispute Bill Gates's importance to the computer world. He has helped create a technological revolution. When historians look back on the twentieth century, they will undoubtedly rank Bill Gates as one of its most influential people.

SOURCES

8   Bill Gates, "Bill Gates's Memo to Employees," Press Release, <http://www.microsoft.com> September 3, 1998.

12 Bill Gates, *The Road Ahead* (New York: Viking, 1995), 172.

12 Stephen Manes and Paul Andrews, *Gates* (New York: Doubleday, 1993), 16.

13 Walter Isaacson, "In Search of the Real Bill Gates, "*Time*, January 13, 1997, 47.

15 Manes and Andrews, 24.

16 Isaacson, 47.

18 Gates, 1.

20 Isaacson, 48.

21 Gates, 18.

21 Ibid.

23 Ibid.

24 Ibid., 290–91.

28 Isaacson, 48.

43 Wallace and Erickson, *Hard Drive: Bill Gates and the Making of the Microsoft Empire* (New York: John Wiley and Sons, 1992), 250.

46 Brent Schlender, "What Bill Gates Really Wants," *Fortune*, January 16, 1995, n. p.

51 Manes and Andrews, 342.

58 Gates, 327.

58 Bill Gates, "The Fascinating Interplay of Biotechnology and Computers," <http://www.microsoft.com> October 21, 1997.

59 Alan Deutschman, "Bill Gates' Next Challenge," *Fortune*, December 28, 1992, 35.

61 Gates, 327.

63 "Bill Gates," *Arts and Entertainment Network, Biography Series*, videotape, ABC News Production and A & E Television Network, 1998, 50 minutes.

68 David Ellis, "Love Bytes: Computer Whiz Bill Gates Ends His Reign as America's Richest Bachelor," *People Weekly*, January 17, 1994, n. p.

72 "The William H. Gates Foundation," <http://www.
microsoft.com> September 3, 1998.

73 Gates, 1.

73–74 Bill Gates, "The Future of Communications," <http://www.
microsoft.com> n. d.

74 Bill Gates, "Ask Bill," <http:www.microsoft.com> January
17, 1995.

76 Michael J. Miller, "Interview: Bill Gates, Microsoft," *PC
Magazine*, March 25, 1997, 233.

76–77 Brent Schlender, "Whose Internet Is It Anyway?" *Fortune*,
December 11, 1995, 126.

84 Isaacson, 51.

84 "Bill Gates," A & E videotape.

86 Leonard Kniffel, "Gates Expands Access Mission during
Alabama Visit," *American Libraries*, April 1998, n. p.

86–87 Evan St. Lifer, "Gates Speaks to Libraries," *Library
Journal*, July 1997, 45.

87 Jean Seligman, "Now an Anti-trust Violation?" *Newsweek*,
February 16, 1998, 64.

89 "Chairman Gates, Up Close and Personal," *U.S. News and
World Report*, October 19, 1998, 15.

90 "Microsoft CEO Bill Gates Sees PC in 60 Percent of U.S.
Homes in 2001," Press Release, <http://www.microsoft.
com> July 29, 1998.

95 Bill Gates, "Column," <http://www.microsoft.com> August
27, 1997.

98 Miller, 233.

101 Brent Schlender, "On the Road with Chairman Bill,"
Fortune, May 26, 1997, 81.

100 Gates, 418.

100 Judge Thomas P. Jackson, "Microsoft Antitrust Trial
Findings of Fact," <http://www.news.findlaw.com/
microsoft.html> January 5, 2000.

100 Michael J. Martinez, "New Roles Seem to Be a Natural
Fit for Microsoft's Leaders," *Associated Press*, January
14, 2000.

GLOSSARY

bug: a flaw in a computer program

CD-ROM: compact disc with read-only memory; a compact disc containing graphics, sound, text, or other data that can be read by a computer

chip: an integrated circuit; a tiny piece of silicon holding the network of electronic components that form the "brains" of a computer

code: a set of instructions for a computer

digital: information stored as numbers

download: to transfer data from a computer or the Internet to another computer

e-mail: electronic mail; messages sent and received between computers linked by telephone lines

graphical user interface (GUI): a computer program that allows a user to interact easily with the computer, typically by using a mouse to make choices from menus or groups of icons

hardware: the physical components of a computer

hypertext markup language (HTML): a computer language used to create web pages

icon: a graphic symbol on a computer screen that represents an application, file, or command

Internet: an electronic communications network that connects many computers around the world

language: a system of computer communication with specific rules and vocabulary

mainframe computer: a large, powerful computer used by a business or institution to perform multiple tasks

mouse: a small mobile device that allows users to control a computer's cursor and to select icons and items from menus

on-line: connected to or available through a computer network

operating system: software that controls the primary operations of a computer and directs the processing of programs

PC: personal computer; a small desktop computer designed to be used by a single person

program: coded instructions for running a specific computer operation

software: the programs and procedures associated with a computer system

spreadsheet: a computer accounting program

Teletype: a machine used to communicate, via telephone lines, with a mainframe computer

web: the World Wide Web; the global network of Internet sites and pages

word processing: the creation and editing of documents on a computer

WYSIWYG: "What You See Is What You Get"; a computer display that exactly reflects the printed document

Selected Bibliography

Books

Gates, Bill. *Business @ the Speed of Thought*. New York: Warner Books, 1999.

Gates, Bill (with Nathan Myrvold and Peter Rinearson). *The Road Ahead*. New York: Viking, 1995.

Ichbiah, Daniel, and Susan L. Knepper. *The Making of Microsoft*. Rocklin, California: Prima Publishing, 1991.

Lowe, Janet. *Bill Gates Speaks*. New York: John Wiley and Sons, 1998.

Manes, Stephen, and Paul Andrews. *Gates: How Microsoft's Mogul Reinvented an Industry—and Made Himself the Richest Man in America*. New York: Doubleday, 1993.

Wallace, James. *Overdrive: Bill Gates and the Race to Control Cyberspace*. New York: John Wiley and Sons, 1997.

Wallace, James, and Jim Erickson. *Hard Drive: Bill Gates and the Making of the Microsoft Empire*. New York: John Wiley and Sons, 1992.

Magazine Articles

Isaacson, Walter. "In Search of the Real Bill Gates." *Time,* January 13, 1997, 44–56.

Miller, Michael J. "Interview: Bill Gates, Microsoft." *PC Magazine,* March 25, 1997, 230–34.

Schlender, Brent. "What Bill Gates Really Wants." *Fortune,* January 16, 1995, 34–47.

On-Line Publications

Jackson, Judge Thomas Penfield. "Microsoft Antitrust Trial Findings of Fact," *Findlaw Library,* November 5, 1999, <http://news.findlaw.com/microsoft.html> January 5, 2000.

"Microsoft Museum," <http://www.microsoft.com/mnscorp/museum>

"Ask Bill Gates," <http://www.askbill@microsoft.com>

"Gates Learning Foundation," <http://www.gatesfoundations.org>

INDEX

OTHER TITLES FROM LERNER AND A&E®:

Arthur Ashe

Bruce Lee

Chief Crazy Horse

Christopher Reeve

George Lucas

Gloria Estefan

Jacques Cousteau

Jesse Owens

Jesse Ventura

John Glenn

Legends of Dracula

Louisa May Alcott

Madeleine Albright

Maya Angelou

Mother Teresa

Nelson Mandela

Princess Diana

Queen Cleopatra

Rosie O'Donnell

Saint Joan of Arc

Wilma Rudolph

Women in Space

Women of the Wild West

ABOUT THE AUTHOR

Jeanne M. Lesinski lives in Ohio and works as a writer and editor for book and magazine publishers all over the country. She has written hundreds of factual sketches for reference books. She enjoys gardening and surfing the net.